MW01257983

FIELD NOTES VOLUME ONE

A. Richardson & R. Skelton
Xylem Books 2018

XY01 The Look Away (2018)
XY02 Field Notes, Volume One (2018)

Field Notes, Volume One

First published in 2012 by Corbel Stone Press
This edition copyright © Xylem Books 2018

ISBN: 978-1-9999718-1-6

Xylem Books is an imprint of Corbel Stone Press

The original 2012 volume of *Field Notes* gathered
together the first four out-of-print titles from the
Corbel Stone Press pamphlet series of the same
name, and added a new collection, *The Flowering
Rock*, written in The Burren on the west coast of
Ireland. For this Xylem Books reissue we have added
Wolf Notes, which was omitted from the first edition
as the original pamphlet was still in print.

The aim of the series is to enshrine an aspect

of a particular place within a single poem or small
collection. In the case of *Typography of the Shore*,
Tentsmuir beach was visited for only a single day,
whereas others, such as the St. Helen's Wood of
Induviæ, were visited many times over a period
of months. It is our hope that each work distills
something of what is unique to each place, whilst
also hinting at the underlying connections that
exist between them.

TYPOGRAPHY OF THE SHORE

A. Richardson & R. Skelton
20th December, 2008
Tentsmuir, Scotland

shell casts in sand

empty presses

birds track salt lines in
tidal measures

footnotes

addenda

marginal scrawl

bracketed between
strand and drift

struck through

by sea

at the margins of the sea
behind the drag of tide
fetched up – departed

heaped broken reeds

vertebral dregs

clotted feathers

bladderwrack and

driftwood strands

shards of mussel

glass and wire

skull of small bird –

spine still clinging

light limned around

orphan pools

revenants

on the fossil shore

desiccated

remaindered

stricken

bleached

exposed

prone

etched

brittle

hallowed

fleeting

forgotten

ragged shoreline
spurred stems ascending
brome and fescue
wind-kerned grasses

matted

threshed

bridled

thefted

winnowed

burnished

and in the surface of the water
a corresponding shirr

for every hare's tail

its answer

infaunal creatures
ebb-drawn to
ferine surfaces

become the
carrion of
sands

.

SKIN & HEATHER

R. Skelton
2005–2008
Anglezarke, England

a threshold

a moment of transition

climb the small stile

gather the small stream

leaves and water

the constant polyphony

moors like scar tissue

skin and heather

ghosts of buildings

families of shadows

a fissure

a feather

a gradual surrender

to stones, dirt and grasses

receive the river

its sudden lulls

without weight

or consequence

forming

binding

dismantling

everything you ever knew

INDUVIÆ

A. Richardson
September–November, 2008
St. Helen's Wood, England

The unattended stones   the tumbled
walls   a path sickled through grasses.

i. A forgotten field

Skeletal rays of hogweed,
dried blood of sorrel,
earthnut,
yarrow –

marrrowless husks;
lushness pared down
to vegetal bones.

The remains of umbellifers.

Desiccated stems / withered leaves.

Seed-heads bend beneath winds.
Stands of fireweed chafe to a shine
in the sun's last light –

a field of corpses
they sway, rise, sigh;

The wind through panicles, coarse-throated;
cough of burr, achene, through nightshade, yarrow.

ætheric imprints still hovering,
flesh departed,

roots still pumping,
hoarding light
into the cellaring cold.

Frayed / bowed / swept / mown.

ii. Wood notes, October 8th, 2008

Sitting in the leaf-litter
I watch
antennæ hunt through
the undergrowth
drift through loam
erupt from the inner
ridgings of bark.

Seeking, dowsing, foraging.

iii. Wood notes, October 18th, 2008

> Saprotrophs bloom
> bloodless from
> the skins of others;
> they harrow
> a mouldering bole
> (supine now
> heartwood cored
> flesh for ants and
> larvæ).

Constellating bark and deadfall.

iv. Wood notes, October 27th, 2008

Birch saplings crowd
the understorey
lean into green pockets of light
leech with weed-vigour
from the nourishing dead.

v. Into November

> I sense the downward cycling,
> the saps' decline,
>
> the descent into root-ways,
> tuber-ways.

The waning. Leaves mould into loam,

fold over seeds and roots.

The sky sags round-bellied with rain.

The stream-bed swells;
waters bruise through ribs of soil,

cough up leaves of oak and
beech, torn stalks of bracken,
wind-culled branches.

Winter rains / winds. Disarticulations / sloughings.

The wax of life recedes, curls into rest.

Caches drip-feed roots, seeds, shoots;
blood in the dens of the slumbering.

vi. Wood notes, November 17th, 2008

The wood rests
(sloughed frayed torn).

A hold for the fallen
(secretly vital).

INTO THE BARE MOORLAND

R. Skelton
May, 2010
The West Pennine Moors, England

Into the bare moorland
unhindered
nature will remake
again

Let the moorland
go to bracken
and others
will follow

Furze and broom
they come after bracken
thriving
to make a richer soil

Furze will reach outwards
dying at its heart
and into its remnants
rowan and birch will seed

They are edge trees
and in time will make
a place for oak and
ash and pine

Let the moorland
go to bracken
and others
will follow

WOLF NOTES

A. Richardson & R. Skelton
January, 2009–March, 2010
Ulpha Fell, England

Stone folded into stone. Familial bonds.
Ice carvings. Water gatherings.
Worm shells. Brakes and mosses.

Wolfhou [1279]

Ulfhou [1337]

Ulpho [1449]

Ulpha [1625]

Ulfay [1646]

Ulpha [1777]

A dark rain of ash above
grasses
fence the unattended stones
the tumbled wall
a path.

Sheer by *Brant Rake.*
Quick by *Hare Gill.*

Brush by *Storthes Gill.*
Pale by *White Moss.*

Ash by *Hesk Fell.*
Dark by *Water Crag.*

Shade by *Fox Bield.*
Marked by *Gray Stone.*

Grasses, sedge and bracken
recover the rootless
felled expanses.

They break ground
for birch, for oak –

finding tenure in a
skin of soil.

Stone packed into stone. Rough
cradle for heather, for bracken.

Black crags insinuated with
stone-crop and rock-rose.

A region for crows, for storm,
tenanted by *meadow* and *quaking* and *blue;*

A waste of blades forged in
sunlight and wind.

A LIST OF PROBABLE GRASSES

Common Bent Grass *Agrostis tenuis,*
Silvery Hair-grass *Aira caryophyllea,*
Early Hair-grass *Aira praecox,*
Sweet Vernal-grass *Anthoxanthum*
odoratum, Fern Grass *Catapodium*
rigidum, Blue Moor-grass *Sesleria*
caerulea, Common Quaking-grass
Briza media, Wavy Hair-grass
Deschampsia flexuosa, Fine-leaved
Sheep's Fescue *Festuca tenuifolia,*
Brome Fescue *Vulpia bromoides,*
Sheep's Fescue *Festuca ovina,* Strong
Creeping Red Fescue *Festuca rubra*
rubra, Annual Meadow-grass *Poa*
annua, Tufted or Meadow Soft-
grass *Holcus lanatus,* Purple Moor-
grass *Molinia caerulea,* Mat-grass
Nardus stricta, Smooth Meadow-
grass *Poa pratensis.*

Duvokeswater c. [1205]

Duuokwat [1279]

Duffokiswatir [c. 1280]

Devoke [1626]

Dovic Water [1769]

Devocke Water [1860]

NEAR WATNESS COY

Alone –
the woven isle.

A clutch for roots and spires within
ever-changing waters.
A last arboreal hold before barren slopes.

The last stand of all that's fallen.

Set like seeds into the fell
above the little dark are stones –

gray weights within a sea of
whins and reeds.

*

Beneath rest those of
an earth once birched,

and their forests, fallen,
feed the roots of grasses.

Raised above *Devoke Water.*
Along *Water Crag, Pike How*
   and *Hall Beck.*

Scattered above *High Ground.*
along *Ladder Crag, Rough Crag*
   and *White Wall.*

Left below *The Seat.*
along *Sike Moss, Brown Rigg*
   and *Crosby Gill.*

GIFT

Where
the rowan grows through
touch, fissures become

becks rivulets gills

shimmed with light, as snow
gives way to sun.

Gorse is the Ever-flower
    wedded to waste places.

Heather is the Brush-flower
    dry sea of violet.

Yew is the Stone-clasp
    reconciled to stone.

Bracken is the Red-wrack
    cast upon the fells.

Haugr, the grave mound, hill or heel
dim shape of rest.

Sker, the isolated rock, peak or cliff
broken face of grey.

Fjall, the mountain, height or moor
high tumbling meadow.

Bekkr, the stream or little river
small rain in the narrow ravine.

No voice but in the tongues
of others
no weight but in the pull
of mountains

> *placeless*
> *breath-stealer*
> *never dwelling*

a form less
clothed than air
tirelessly stitching-unstitching
hill side, moor and fell.

Host to revenant skins –
departed stands of birch

and oak and holly – their bones
became the birthing saps for grasses.

Now this terrestrial sea.
These stalks wave-shaped by winds

decay and ready the earth
for birch again.

Harter Fell, a memory;
    the hill bereft of deer.

Birker Fell, an echo;
    the hill absented by birch.

Ulpha Fell, a reproach;
    the hill silenced of wolves.

THE BRIGHT ONE

The beginning; the inception;
the medicine stirrings of earth.

*

The rowan seed, cased
in cold soils, stirs; a tiny
fist unfurls – muscles
upwards – piercing crust.
A translucent filament seeks
the sun. Sips from melting drifts.

THE FLOWERING ROCK

A. Richardson & R. Skelton
March–September, 2010
The Burren, County Clare, Ireland

From the water   they rise and fall
blue hills breathing   songs without words.

Each morning
and the sounds of birds,

of wind
and water.

Each morning
and the ever-changing hues of the sea –

its manifold greys,
browns, greens and blues.

Down on the shattered rocks

madder
and thrift

eyebright
and hart's-tongue

blooming minutiæ.

The scars hold life

are living seams of green,
amber, cerulean, rose.

Spring gentian,
  ceadharlach bealtaine;

blackthorn,
  draighean (wretched one; penetrator);

sea spleenwort,
  fionncha mara;

bitter vetch,
  corra meille (crane's pea);

cowslip,
  bainne bó bleachtáin (milk of the milch cow);

herb robert,
  eireaball rí (tail of the king);

wild garlic,
  gairleóg;

primrose,
  sabhaircín (delight, pleasure);

dog violet,
  fanaigse (fragile weed);

early-purple orchid,
  magairlín meidhreach.

The walls have vacancies,
interstices, vents –
they seem a pale net-work;
knots of grey rope
staked out to
land the great catch.

Those weir-men who
stitched them, laid them,
have long gone, down
within the hills' pores,
but whether by luck
or design the walls
stand still, whilst haw
and rowan heave and sigh,
catching the wind's
ceaseless expirations.

.

Listen.
A low, muted,
bell-like sound.

They are *na clocha clingeacha* –
the ringing stones –
the bell stones.

Tread lightly.
Remember their voices
amongst the rocks.

First

the hooked mouth
of the sea

second

the drill
of the water

third

the bleat
of the heather

fourth

the dwarf
of the earth

fifth

the head
of the copse

sixth

the cut-throat
of the hedge

seventh

the little singer
of the willow

eighth

the clacker
of the gorse.

As the sea retreats
a way opens

to the blackened rocks
of an ancient and natural corridor.

The oldest, most enduring,
and yet most insubstantial road.

More ancient than bohreens,
than green roads, drove roads.

Commuted by heron, oystercatcher
and snipe. Forested by sea-oak.

Carpeted by red and green
and brown.

And beyond the shore –

    ghost islets
              emerge,
    glimmer briefly,

then resubmerge –
revenants
of the waves.

Avens, thorn and fern
prostrate juniper
fold into fissures
harbour within stone

and beneath

arterial passages
underground flows
wailing notes
of water and wind

the hollow songs
of hollow hills.

blue   grey   violet

              fissured   scarred   eroded

fluted   caved   porous

              rill-worn   costal   yielding

Along the shattered pavement
are *scailps* (clefts, fissures, grikes) –
joints and seams prized open
over millennia –
the tireless work of water
(of acids and gravity)
as it flows
towards the
resurgent
stream.

An old way
has turned to greening

returned to bloodwort
crane's-bill
and meadowsweet

ending in a hazel wood
thickening over forgotten fields.

Here grey walls have fallen

succumbed to roots and
the steady perambulations of rain

to hawthorn and bramble
winding through heartstones.

Elders bloom
throughout the aged garden

(planted by hands for fever –
for breathing through a long winter)

and nettles
have reclaimed the hearth.

The medicine remains
(needing neither roads nor hands)
engulfing the traces left

returning furrow and field
to wild meadow and woodland.

Milkwort,
>   *lus an bhainne;*

silverweed,
>   *briosclán* (brittle one);

hawthorn,
>   *sceach gheal* (white haw);

sea campion,
>   *coireán mara;*

bloody crane's-bill,
>   *crobh dearg* (red talon);

sea pink,
>   *rabhán;*

sanicle,
>   *bodán coille;*

common butterwort
>   *bodán meascáin;*

wild strawberry,
>   *sú talún;*

wall rue,
>   *luibh na seacht ngábh* (the seven signs herb).

Through narrow rooms,
along the small lengths
of stone corridors, passages, precincts

      birds   *glimmer*

alight on jutting tongues of stone
(from the open
mouths of rock fissures)
find resting chambers,
a moment's pause,
a brief dimming.

Pulled along
unseen, familial lines,
the bird glides
heavily
with rigid, graceless wings.

Eventually it will ground,
this grey, silent kite.

It cannot endure on memory
and repulsion alone.

This shy bird is *corr réisc,*
the marsh bill,
but it could equally be called
an dealbh srutha,
the river statue,
or *an chloch a stánann,*
the gaze stone –
crouching, motionless,
on the furthest reaches of the boat cove.

But sometimes
it breaks its vow of silence –
a premonitory, piercing cry.

And then truly it earns the name
corr scréachóg,
or screech heron.

And further up the shore,
a white kestrel
hovers over the waters.
Seabhac mara.
A watcher of forms
beneath the blue-green
glass. A sudden diver
into the shifting tide.

Time after time
it makes a knot in the sky,
holding the fury
of the air at bay
with slow wing beats,
waiting
for a glint
of silver below.

The physic garden. Four centuries derelict.

Rosemary

feverfew

vervain

dog-rose

wormwood

ramsons

mint

flourish still. The elder has seeded a small wood.

Seeking a desert
they came to these blue stones.

Seeking desolation
they found instead the flowering rock.

Devil's-bit scabious,
   odhrach bhallach;

bird's-foot trefoil,
   crobh éin (bird talon);

yarrow,
   athair thalún (ground father);

carline thistle,
   feochadáin mín (fine thistle);

wall lettuce,
   leitís bhalla;

wood sage,
   iúr sléibhe (mountain yew);

selfheal,
   duán ceannchosach;

wild thyme,
   tím chreige;

lady's bedstraw,
   boladh cnis (the scent of skin);

harebell,
   méaracán púca (goblin's thimble).

There is a clamour
down by the sea.

Gulls congregate
on the narrow islets
just beyond the promontory.

Common,
black-headed,
lesser black-backed,
greater black-backed.

And mingled in
with the laridæn chatter –
the fraught piping of the curlew,
and the plaintive, solitary
calling of the oystercatcher.

Do they sense the downward cycle too?
The turn away from the sun.
The descent into autumn.

Muich,
> sadness, dullness; a mist, a fog;

murchortha,
> things thrown ashore by the sea;

murdhuach,
> a mermaid, a sea-nymph;

murdhubhchaill,
> a cormorant (black sea hag);

murgabhal,
> an arm of the sea;

murmar,
> a murmur, noise of talk or of the sea;

murse,
> sea-shore, sea-marsh;

murthol,
> tide, flowing of the sea;

murthoradh,
> produce of the sea;

toichim,
> going, departing.

From the water
they are adrift

blue hills, dark with rain.

What the stones enfold
remains their own.

What the tide pulls away
returns transformed

if it returns at all.

If the liver has a sound
it will be this sound –

the drag and suck of waves

waters filtering through weed
through sand

tirelessly, tirelessly
swabbing shore-stones

turning grit to glass.

NOTES

2. TYPOGRAPHY OF THE SHORE : First published in 2009 by
   Corbel Stone Press.
5. *Cast*, the mould used to make metal type; PRESS, i.e.
   letterpress, the means of marking a page with metal or
   wooden type.
6. *Track*, (in typography) the action of adjusting the spacing
   between letters and words; *measure*, a means of determining
   proportions; also, metre, or units of rhythm in poetry.
7. *Struck through*, deleted by means of a straight line
   through a word.
10. *Ragged*, unjustified type; a region of type in which one
    margin is kept unaligned; *spur*, a serif-like ending to the
    stroke of a letterform; *stem*, the main, usually vertical,
    stroke of a letterform; *ascender*, the upward projecting
    stem of a lowercase letter, such as 'b' or 'd'; *brome*, a grass
    of the genus Bromus; *fescue*, a genus of tufted grass;
    kerned, the action of adjusting the spacing between pairs
    of letterforms; *shirr*, drawn together; a gather in the
    texture of a fabric.
11. *Hare's tail*, a coastal species of grass; *tail*, the descending,
    often ornamental, stroke of a letterform.
12. *Infaunal*, dwelling within sediment; *ferine*, wild, feral.
14. SKIN & HEATHER : First published in 2010 by Corbel Stone
    Press. Collaged from *Landings* – Skelton's book about the
    West Pennine Moors of northern England.
28. INDUVIÆ : First published in 2010 by Corbel Stone Press.
    Induviæ are the withered leaves that cling to the stem of
    some plants; not falling; remaining for some time.
33. *Umbellifer*, of a family of plants, usually aromatic with
    hollow stems, producing clusters of radiating compound
    flower-heads, known as umbels. Examples include:
    angelica, carrot, hogweed, parsley, hemlock and chervil.

34. *Panicle*, re: grasses: a flower-head which is borne on stalks, which are in turn borne upon branches from the main stem. Also: any branched inflorescence.

37. *Saprotroph*, an organism (such as the fungus Sulphur Tuft, *Hypholoma fasciculare*) which derives its nourishment from dead or decaying organic matter.

40. *Disarticulation*, to become disjointed, esp. the bones of a body or the stems of a plant.

44. INTO THE BARE MOORLAND : First published in 2010 by Corbel Stone Press. Written in absentia, in Ireland, after reading a passage from *The Permaculture Way* by Graham Bell.

54. WOLF NOTES : First published in late 2010 by Corbel Stone Press in a very limited, two volume 'folio' edition with supplementary texts, followed by a larger, single volume edition in 2011. *Wolf Notes* is a sequence for the Cumbrian uplands between the Duddon Valley and Eskdale, later expanded into a series of booklets and collected in the volume, *Memorious Earth,* ISBN 978-0-9572121-7-6.

58. *Wolfhou, etc,* a partial toponymic sequence for the place-name Ulpha, from the Old Norse *Ulfr haugr,* interpreted by modern scholars, including Diana Whaley, as 'hill of the wolf'.

62. *Meadow, quaking, blue,* the grasses *Poa annua, Briza media* and *Sesleria caerulea.*

64. *Duvokeswater, etc,* a partial toponymic sequence for the place-name Devoke Water, possibly from the Brittonic **dubáco* or **dubácá,* meaning 'the dark one'.

66. *The little dark,* the tarn, Devoke Water.

73. *Harter Fell,* from the Old Norse *hjartar fjall,* 'mountain of the hart or stag'; *Birker Fell,* from the Old Norse *birki erg fjall,* 'mountain of the shieling by the birch trees'.

76. THE FLOWERING ROCK : First published in 2012 in
    Field Notes (Volume One) by Corbel Stone Press, ISBN
    978-0-9572121-0-7.

95. *Corr réisc,* the common Irish name for the grey heron,
    which translates as 'marsh bill'. Both *river statue* and *gaze
    stone* are coinages – many thanks to Caoimhín MacGiolla
    Léith, as elsewhere in this collection, for translating them
    into Irish; *Corr scréachóg,* 'screech heron', is curiously
    enough a folk-name for the screech or barn owl, found
    in Dinneen's dictionary, which also mentions *corr
    scréacha, corr scréadóige* and simply *scréachóg.* Here *corr
    scréachóg* has been reappropriated for the heron.

96. *Seabhac mara,* Irish for 'sea hawk'. This, and *white kestrel,*
    are coinages for an unknown bird of the gull family, seen
    fishing just off the shore by Ballyconry.

97. Written for the ruins of Corcomroe Abbey, a Cistercian
    monastery in County Clare; *physic garden,* part of a
    monastic garden used for growing medicinal herbs.

99. *Laridæn,* from Laridæ, the gull family.

100. *Muich,* etc, Irish words gathered from the dictionaries of
     O'Reilly and Dinneen.

TEXTS

The Permaculture Way
Graham Bell, 2004

British Flora
Gaston Bonnier, 1925

The Gaelic Names of Plants
John Cameron, 1883

Cairns of the Birker Fell and Ulpha Fell Area
J. Cherry, 1961

A Thesaurus of Bird Names
Michel Desfayes, 1998

The Place-Names of Cumberland
Bruce Dickins, 1950

*A Glossary of Words and Phrases
Pertaining to the Dialect of Cumberland*
William Dickinson, 1878

Foclóir Gaedhilge agus Béarla
Patrick S. Dinneen, 1927

*Ring Cairns to Reservoirs: Archaeological
Discoveries in the Duddon Valley, Cumbria*
Duddon Valley Local History Group, 2009

The Place-Names of Lancashire
Eilert Ekwall, 1922

Irish Trees
Niall Mac Coitir, 2003

A Supplement to the Glossary
of the Dialect of Cumberland
E.W., Prevost, 1905

The Burren, A Companion to the
Wildflowers of an Irish Limestone Wilderness
E. Charles Nelson & Wendy Walsh, 1997

Wild Plants of The Burren and the Aran Islands
Charles Nelson, 2008

An Irish-English Dictionary
Edward O'Reilly, 1864

Landings
Richard Skelton, 2009

A Dictionary of Lake District Place-Names
Diana Whaley, 2006